"Make Money Online Methods"

How to make money online and generate passive incomes

Presented By Amy D Morse

Click to Access

Check out this money making resource before you continue !

"Simply Copy & Paste" !

Click here to see This now

Table of contents

Recommended Resources

How to Make Money Online Fast In Today's Economy

Genuine Ways Of Making Money Online

Legitimate Ways to Make Money Online Fast

How to Make Money Online With Craigslist.

Make Money On YouTube

Make money online with CPA offers.

Make money with Drop shipping

Make Money Selling Ebooks Online With Unique Marketing Strategy!

Highly Recommended Resources

Recommended Resources

[“Simply Copy & Paste” !](#)

[Make Residual](#)

[CB Passive Income](#)

[Make $2000 Monthly on You tube](#)

[PLR Niche Guru](#)

[$1200 Cash Profit](#)

[Earn $1000 in 24 hours](#)

[Make Money with Facebook](#)

How to Make Money Online Fast In Today's Economy

Are you a victim of today's economy, and in desperate need of a dependable income?

The need to learn how to make money online fast is all too common for many people today. There are several reasons why this issue resonates with so many.

These reasons include, job loss, pay-checks too small to cover living expenses, the desire to spend more time with your family, the desire to be your own boss.

And maybe the most powerful reason of all is the desire to create the lifestyle of your dreams, based on financial independence.

Of course, there is a secret to making money online fast. And the secret is to have laser-like focus on your objective.

Bruce Lee summarized this "secret" in a powerful quote:

"The Successful Warrior is the Average Man, With Laser-like Focus."

Notice that Bruce Lee did not say the "exceptional man.

" He states clearly that the average person, meaning any man or woman can be a "successful warrior," a successful online entrepreneur. All they need is laser-like focus

So how Do You Achieve Laser-like Focus?

The starting point is to define your objective.

Do you want to supplement your current paycheck? Do you want to spend more time with your family? Do you want to be your own boss? Or, do you want to create the lifestyle of your dreams?

You must answer these questions with complete honesty. After all, no one is listening. This is all in your private world.

A couple of these questions overlap a bit. However, it's important that you answer them as you truly feel deep inside, because this will be the driving force that will propel you to success.

Once you've identified you true motive, you can do some research to identify a profitable business model that you can develop the laser-like focus on.

Profitable Business Model

Without a profitable business model you will fail online. This may sound harsh, but it's true.

There are numerous profitable business models you can choose, such as Internet marketing (teaching people how to make money online), affiliate marketing, blogging, providing services, such as writing quality content for online entrepreneurs.

This last one is excellent for people who need immediate cash to cover bills, or to provide the limited working capital necessary to get an online business off the ground.

Educate Yourself

Once you have identified your profitable business model, you can research how best to educate yourself on your chosen business model. There are countless courses available online. Many of them are junk, which is often characterized by nonsense hype.

However, there are a number of reputable, successful online marketers who offer proven training courses in your chosen business model. Be very selective in your choice. Remember, if it sounds too good to be true, 9 times of 10, it is.

Personal Business Coach

For your best chance at early success, get a successful, personal business coach. They don't come cheap, but if you want to achieve success fast, this is the surest way I know.

An experienced personal business coach will save you time AND money in the long run, because they will guide you past many pitfalls and false starts. These are not only wasteful, but they can be heartbreaking. They may cause you to give up.

Are you beginning to see now how your laser-like focus

can ensure your success making money online fast, not matter what your starting point is?

I confess, I am obsessed with traffic. That's because after years of frustration trying to get traffic to my websites, I've discovered the power of some easy, time-tested methods for FREE, and low-cost traffic generation.

Check out this money making resource before you continue !

"Simply Copy & Paste" !
Click here to see This now

Genuine Ways Of Making Money Online

Earning money online is not that difficult until we can find the exact sites to earn money online. Also there are different ways of online earning opportunities among which some are more popular than other.

Earning Money Writing Articles:-

Right now there are many sites which provide money for writing articles. Articles may be related to anything. Some sites gives money for writing particular types of articles and some accept any types of articles. Some sites provide information regarding the topic for writing the article. Some people make this as a full time business too.

Generally writing articles is not that easy job and needs a lot of practice. Article writing is something like a boon which can be achieved but you need to follow some rules and regulations. This makes your articles more attractive and people don't get bored while reading.

Now coming to the payment, some sites after submitting articles gives offer for your articles and asks whether you like it or not. Some sites informs the money you are going to get before you write articles and some sites gives money according to the number of visitors for your article.

Earning Money Completing surveys:-

Surveys are a set of queries which you need to answer. In general surveys are a series of questions for which you need to give your opinion. Generally earning money through surveys is more in US and Canada because more survey sites are concentrated there. You need to complete your profile in which you need to fill some details like your occupation, hobbies, education status, personal details and lot more. After completing these, you are allotted surveys which match your profile.

Generally each survey varies from $1 to $5. The more money you get for a survey the more time it takes to complete. A typical survey will be around 10 to 15 min. Generally survey sites provide individual payouts, i.e. if you earn $2 for a survey your pay-pal account will be updated with that money. But some survey sites keep a minimum payout and after reaching that minimum threshold you will be allotted checks.

Earn money writing reviews:-

This is also another popular way of earning money. Here you need to register with the companies first before writing reviews. Generally companies want reviews about products that are new to market as people need to know about the product. More review sites like reviews related to computers, mobiles, gadgets etc. as they are the more fast moving products.

So coming to the pay that you will be getting for each review will be around $2. Some sites give incentives and some sites give both straight money and also incentives too. Right now this is also a very good opportunity for earning money.

Earn Money Through Blogging:-

This is one of the most popular way of earning money online. Though this is the toughest way of earning money which takes more time to earn, this is best way of earning money. For the first few months until your site gets some traffic you will not be getting any money from your blog. That will be a very hard time until your blog gets some popularity. Once the blog gets popular then people can start earning money.

Right now its hard to find good blogs because they need to be updated regularly. Generally developing blogs need some patience. Once the patience was lost its difficult to maintain the blog. Generally blog owners, from the starting of the blog try to earn money since the blog has started and if they can't earn then they loose interest and the blog automatically dies. So, it's something like a business which needs more patience.

Earn Money By Affiliate Marketing:-

Affiliates are something like a part of a company and the way affiliate marketing works is simple. You need to promote the products they give and if people buy those products from you, then you will be given some percentage in the sale. This is one of the difficult businesses but which can produce shower of dollars if you know the secret. Right now on the internet there are very good tutorials for learning the tricks. So this is also a good way to earn but right now there is a big competition to make money like this. Hence if you are opting then you will enter into a fierce competition and if stand top from the peers then you can see the full time earning opportunity and you can quit your job.

Earn Money Participating In Forums:-

This is also a part of online earning opportunities, which is gaining its craze in the last few months. Right now there are many forums which are giving money for participating. So people are participating in many forums at the same time so all the collected earnings will give you handsome amount of money. But for writing in forums some rules should be followed. If they are not followed then the administrator of the forums will ban the accounts. Hence if the rules are followed correctly then its easy to earn money from these forums. Right now we can earn simultaneously in three ways at the same time actively participating in forums.

It is sure a very good part time and even can convert to a full time if you are to totally dedicate.

So these are most prominent ways of earning money online from which making big money is possible. Hence visit this site to know more about Online Earning Opportunities and also sites which helps you in making money online.

Check out this money making resource before you continue !

"Simply Copy & Paste" !

Click here to see This now

LEARN HOW TO MAKE $2,000 PER MONTH ON YOUTUBE WITH NO FILMING! CLICK HERE TO LEARN HOW

Legitimate Ways to Make Money Online Fast

You are probably familiar with the prospect of earning money online. Perhaps you have even tried it yourself, but were unsuccessful and hoping to seek some advice. Well, the truth is, earning money online is entirely possible, but requires a lot of dedication and hard work, with just a hint of luck. Below are listed some of the possible ways to make money online.

1. **Selling Stuff Online**

Selling things online can be done by anyone and opens up so many doors. If you have a lot of clutter around your house, you could be sitting on a goldmine. With websites such as eBay and Amazon, it is incredibly easy to sell second-hand items. Albeit you probably won't be earning a lot per item, but if you have hundreds of items, you could easily see your income growing. This is usually only a temporary solution, unless you plan on finding inventory from wholesalers or even creating your own products, such as you will often see on Etsy. More commonly nowadays, many people are selling things on Facebook, since the introduction of groups have made it so easy. Similarly to Craigslist, this is a good option if you prefer selling and buying in your local area.

2. Affiliate Advertising

Affiliate advertising may be something you have heard about, but not a lot of people really understand its purpose. You earn a commission selling products or services for someone else, usually through links on a blog or website. This method can be quite successful when done properly, but it won't make you rich overnight. In order to sell, you need to attract a high amount of traffic to your blog or website, with the appropriate content and information, which will hopefully encourage your readers to use your affiliate links.

3. Work at Home Jobs

This is a large umbrella term used to describe any sort of job that can be done long-distance, or more specifically, from home. While many careers can be done from a home office, some of the most popular ones are data entry, blogging and even doing surveys. Again, these are usually slow-earners, but can give you some supplementary income on the side of your full-time job. Surveys are outsources to a large amount of people, when a company is doing market research, so they are usually run through an organization such as Global Test Market or Toluna. The latter offers a variety of ways to earn extra money, including product testing and polls.

4. Web page Design

Web page design is in huge demand and if you have a computer and an internet connection, you can also learn how to code. With a thorough knowledge of HTML, CSS and PHP, you already have all the tools to build simple web pages. Consider helping others with their WordPress themes, portfolio web pages or blogs, and you could be earning some serious money.

Check out this money making resource before you continue !

"Simply Copy & Paste" !
Click here to see This now

How to Make Money Online With Craigslist.

Craigslist is the best marketplace for buying and selling of products in your local community.

It is a good marketplace to find hot jobs, real estate, books, electronic items or anything you need in your daily life. But it requires lots of skills to make money online with Craigslist, one of most visited classified website on Internet.

Here is how one can make some good amount of money using Craigslist:

1. Submit product or items that you want to see in the proper category. You will not get the benefit if you submit your items in the wrong category and even your entry will be rejected for submitting in the wrong category.

2. Create an eye catching heading for your listing and if possible include an attractive price in your heading section.

Include maximum pictures that you can add about the product you are listing on Craigslist. Listings with pictures perform better compared to only text listings on Craigslist.

Also you can include your e-mail id your listing if you want buyers to contact you about the listing you have added.

3. You should read Craigslist rules and regulations before start submitting your stuff here. Submit a well formatted and error free ad copy on Craigslist. Because if you do something wrong against their policies, you can get blacklisted.

Never try to submit the same ad copy frequently.

You can remain in touch with what other people are posting in your category with AdNotifier.

Use HTML code to direct people to the link from where they can buy the product you have listed on Craigslist.

Follow-up immediately with the buyers who shows interest in your items. Buyers who show interest in your items are surely in the position to buy that item. So don't miss this money making opportunity whenever you get it.

if you are really aiming at making some good amount of money on Craigslist, never do the following:

   4.Never try submitting the same Ad copy over and over

on Craigslist. This way you are just spamming Craigslist

5. Don't post too frequently. If you must do multiple postings, keep a gap of some minutes in your postings.

6. Don't submit your ad copy in the wrong category

7. Don't submit an ad copy with grammatical and formatting errors

8. Avoid including affiliate links in your ad copy.

Check out this money making resource before you continue !

"Simply Copy & Paste" !
Click here to see This now

Make Money On YouTube

YouTube has made video publishing a great way to earn money and also to

promote your business or service globally. It has gained significant popularity as high-quality video recording becomes less expensive. All you need these days is a decent stand-alone camera or one good smart phone and you can create some footage to rival big budget videos. It's all about creativity and a good angle on forging a response from your potential viewers.

The Set-up

Before you begin fancying yourself as the next Danny Boyle, it's best to look into what kind of video you want. Are you looking to make direct money, or are you looking to use your video to promote engagement? Sometimes it's common to be doing this for both reasons. What and why you film and post on YouTube determines the type of content on your uploads. In view of direct or indirect income from your video it's clear that the measure of success is the number of views and shares your video can harvest. So what goes viral? We can never really predict what will, but based on past trends we can make some reasoned guesses. Even if your video doesn't become a global hit, you can still cash in on the camcorder income, and a bit of any extra cash for your trouble.

The Delivery

Depending on the aim of the video, you can gather interest by presenting facts in an authoritative manner to keep the viewer informed or curious, and add external clips that relate to your subject as and when it is appropriate. If you opt for the light-hearted informal approach, keeping your video both entertaining and funny whilst still relating to your area of business is key to its success. Use informative tutorials or 'how to's presented with a tongue-in-cheek attitude to boost your viewing figures. Humour is always a good angle. There are quite a lot of free video editing tools that would make for good graphics for your clip, text sliders and integrated audio is easier to create and add than you think. A videoed opinion works well for direct sales or promotion if it's well put together. Short, sharp and quick is the way ahead. Remember, online viewers have a very short attention span. You have the first 8 seconds to keep the viewer in your space. Start with a bang and maintain interest by editing out any irrelevant bits.

Sell! Sell! Sell!

If you sell a product or service, it pays to get customer testimonials that can be embedded into your website. It goes miles further than text testimonials, as anyone can do a fictitious one in a matter of seconds. This will not only enhance your YouTube representation, but its also useful footage that can be edited into your other venture - a video advert!

If you're introducing a new product or service you could film an instructional video to go with it, giving both your business and your new gadget a boost. Publishers and authors do it all the time. Offer useful information around the subject your product is related to. Tell your viewers things they don't know and then introduce your product without too much of a hard sell.

The dollar shaving club clip is still trending as the benchmark of all YouTube trade-focused videos. A total cost of $3,000 and some jobless members of staff helped Michael Dubin gain over 5 million views and huge volume sales of $1.00 shaving sticks. It's an example of what imagination can do to get your message viral. He gained a huge viewing fan base, but to also gain 3% global sales conversion is nothing short of genius. View the Dollar Shave Club hit.

As a good starting point, make a fun video commercial showcasing your company culture or typical customer scenario. Showing footage of your busy work environment, fulfilling orders or demonstrating the benefits of your business would need entertainment or shock to transform one viewer into 10 or 20. A good video is only great for a single viewer to respond or engage. But to get viral it has to be funny, controversial, or very informative. A video that your viewers share on social networks is what you want. That's the true meaning of a viral attack spread by those exposed to it. We'd advise that traffic by controversy should be left to the professional marketers or those that are just seeking a multitude of viewers and nothing else. It can produce risky results.

For those new to posting on YouTube, it's probably best to be yourself. Be sure to present your unique selling point. As tempting as it is to hire a glamorous blonde as your spokesperson, this tactic usually succeeds in putting people off, so get some real people in front of the camera and let your customers see you can be trusted. Successful videos that have worked like a dream for the originators are typically make-up artists, business coaches, quirky retailers and entertaining web ventures.

Music has also enjoyed commercial exposure on YouTube, and we are not talking about a major artiste or record label. Dub FX was a dub performer plying his trade for a few pounds around Camden and other similar European streets. Footage of his performance on YouTube reached a huge viewing number and, now, let's just say he had his baptism at Glastonbury.

Click And Buy

New media technology doesn't sit idle, especially when it comes to finding ways to create direct sales as you engage with media. Some started the idea with product placement as you watch a clip on YouTube. Now you can actually click on a highlighted object in videos and buy the item through the click through link. The set-up is much cheaper than when the technology was in Beta a few years back. You can have the programme running in your £20 YouTube video for a monthly package. A good way to more or less set up a YouTube shop is to have a scrolling catalogue with audio comment and some interesting footage to keep the viewer interested. Your content should capture the viewer's attention and keep them there. If it's fashion - talk about trends, tips and styles, throw in the odd celebrity picture and then display your items. The same goes for services.

You can have clickable scrolling text as you introduce your unique service. Order now, book your place, and other calls to action phrases can bring you some direct revenue.

Ranking And AdSense

YouTube is great vitamins for your Google health. Search engines and web ranking your web presence can do wonders for surfer engagement and trade. After you've uploaded your video, be sure to enter a title, description and tags. After you've managed your key words and set phrases with supporting descriptions you're on your way to getting a bit of a traffic boost courtesy of Google. Your video should be making a few hundred hits if you harness strategic links and spread the word on your social network or from your website. You video should start appearing on Google, riding on the back of your key phrases. Click-throughs to websites enjoy a healthy percentage from video searches commonly connected to YouTube. Page ranking with the help of your video on YouTube is therefore worthy of great consideration. Do your homework with how AdSense works and revenue from here can be realistic and consistent. Payments are made by YouTube into a Google AdSense account, and once you are fully enrolled in the programme you will also be able to switch on Google ads either to the side of or on top of your videos. This can earn additional income through pay per click and affiliate profits, and all you have to do is keep your video content fresh and enjoy the proceeds. Apart from direct payment, there are other ways you can build up your YouTube reputation to develop other revenue streams. You may be selling a few products on eBay or needing to get more visitors to your revenue-generating blog; it makes sense to include a link back to your site. You can engage with other businesses in your industry and offer to endorse their products in your videos, for a 5-10% commission on top of what YouTube pays you, or simply enter into an affiliate partnership. Do this without the middle men affiliate companies and your commission is yours alone.

The Partner Programme

The Partner Programme is where your videos really start working for you. Once you are a partner, you can expect to earn about $2.50-$5 (£1.56-£3.13) per 1,000 views of your video, and whilst this doesn't sound very much right now, if you do manage to create the next viral sensation that brings in millions of viewings, you can expect to earn quite a dotcom lot for your hard work. Consider making money by selling scrolling text integrated into your video. A certain number of viewers is all the proof needed to have a platform for a related business to be interested. Product placement and endorsements as part of the content is an effective means to promote the business of a paying advertiser, big or small.

Fan Currency

Make your uploads unique and positively different and you are sure to build up a dedicated following of fans. Video marketing is not a get-rich-quick scheme, and to a certain extent it can be unpredictable; patience and thoughtful planning should help. It can be a lot of fun making the videos, and once they do start earning for you, they are likely to continue to do so month on month. Feed your fans, introduce videos from others that have some sort of connection to yours. By the time you've built up a library of 15 or more videos, you should be achieving a good number of views per video. Once all your videos achieve a minimum of 1,000 views each, you are sure to be contacted by YouTube asking if you would like to apply to become a Partner.

LEARN HOW TO MAKE $2,000 PER MONTH ON YOUTUBE WITH NO FILMING! CLICK HERE TO LEARN HOW

Posting videos on YouTube is a very public thing to do. You therefore need to be clear about permission and the terms for posting a video. Play it safe and make sure you have permission where applicable so that you don't find your good work is not a wasted exercise. Situational footage where you bear witness with your video are exempt in some cases, so it's a good idea to know what the parameters to this are. Make sure your video does not infringe someone else's copyright. Take a few minutes and read through YouTube's guidelines. They are also there to protect your own good work from others; you'd need to know when your copyright interests have been subject to infringement too. See YouTube copyright tips and guidance. Making money by way of YouTube has more options than we may be used to. It's all up to you to put some catchy material together and manipulate income once the viewing figures begin to rise. It's an open playground - let's get filming.

Check out this money making resource before you continue !

"Simply Copy & Paste" !

Click here to see This now

Make money online with CPA offers.

CPA marketing is One of the fastest and effective ways to make money online.

It is the most lucrative, if you know how to do it right.

In this article, I will walk you through the 5 steps that you need to know to create successful CPA marketing campaign and make the most money.

Here is the free Free CPA Marketing step by step guide:

Step 1: Join the Best CPA Networks

In order to successfully promote CPA offers and make the most money, first you have to join trusted CPA networks which act as mediators between affiliates and merchants.

That is , if you want to make money using CPA marketing -- you must first join a low risk, reputable and trusted CPA networks.

Step 2: Select Profitable CPA Offer

Once you join CPA network, you should be able to select high converting CPA offer that brings maximum result.

In other words, as proper CPA offers selection is the most critical task in successful CPA marketing, you have to diligently carry out your CPA offer selection tasks as so to find offers that bring the highest success.

Step 3: Test

Once you select CPA offer you should drive traffic to your CPA offer. This is done to test your CPA offer.

Basically, what testing means is that you spend little advertisement budget and effort to test the profitability of CPA offer and marketing technique you use.

You just test, track and optimize until you find a winning formula.

That is, you have to test every thing until you come up with optimum result -- the winning formula.

Step 4: Scale

After you test your campaign using fast traffic generation source like PPC marketing, you need to scale it to other traffic sources.

The good news is that there are lots of ways to promote CPA offers on the Internet.

You will have two options to drive targeted traffic to your CPA offers: Paid and Free.

Paid Options

As it has been noted earlier driving traffic is the life blood idea of any successful CPA marketing campaign.

If you do not have traffic, even with the most profitable offer selection, it is meaning less.

There fore, you have to go where massive targeted traffic exists and capture it.

There are lots of paid ways that can get you traffic.

Some of them are:

1. **PPC Search Engines -- Targeted Traffic Source**
2. **PPV networks -- Targeted Traffic Source**
3. **Other traffic sources** such as MySpace, YouTube,

Facebook advertisement, etc (note: these traffic sources are not targeted, so you need to be careful when advertising)

4. Buying ad space from related forum

Using the above paid traffic generation sources you can get a huge number of visitors to your CPA offers.

But, there are important points that you need to be aware of when using PAID advertisement option.

That is ...

Every time you use any paid advertisement option, start with a small budget - test, track and optimize until you come up with a wining formula. Then after, you massively scale it based on your wining formula.

Ok, now let's see the free options.

There are lots of free ways you can make money using CPA offers.

Some of them are:

* Video marketing
* Articles Marketing
* Yahoo Answers
* Classified Ads, etc.

Step 5: Rinse and Repeat

Once you create a successful CPA marketing campaign, move to another offer and repeat the process again and again.

Conclusion

As CPA marketing is the most lucrative way to make money online, you have to understand how to create and run successful CPA marketing campaign.

The steps laid out above will help you a lot and I highly recommend you to implement them as fast as possible.

Make money with Drop shipping

Drop shipping companies provide an opportunity for you to run a store without actually having to maintain any inventory. They exist for just about every type of product you can imagine. Some provide access to a wide array of products, such as what you would find at your local Wal-Mart or Target. Others provide niche-specific products, such as what you might find at a local Bass Pro Shop.

Find a Drop Shipping Company

Unfortunately, there are plenty of drop shipping opportunities that aren't exactly legit. It's important that you take the time to find a company that has solid reviews from satisfied customers. Avoid any that seem to have a history of scamming their sellers, as these will only result in difficulties with your business in the future.

It's also essential to avoid paying any fee to get started with a drop shipping company. They earn their share of the profits when you sell a product, and any attempt to charge you for the opportunity to work with them should be seen as a red flag.

You should give preference to drop shipping companies that have an integrated shopping cart solution. It will simplify the entire process of setting up your website and help to minimize your expenses. It is also far easier to maintain these sites, as you won't have to deal with adding and deleting products from your store.

Find a Niche and Review the Market for Your New Products

After you find a company that seems to be on the up and up, it's important you match it to a potential niche. Don't just assume that there's a market for the products they're selling simply because they're offering a niche-based opportunity.

A good way to determine whether or not the products you'll be selling are in demand is to check Amazon.com. If you can find similar products that are being reviewed by real customers, then you can be sure that there's a demand. If you can't, it doesn't mean that the market doesn't exist, but it may prove a lot more difficult to actually turn this into a profitable opportunity.

Maintain a Blog and Social Media Presence

It isn't enough to just put together a shopping cart. Customers are unlikely to find it, and even if they do, there's no reason for them to choose your store over a competitors. You can differentiate your business easily, though, with a regularly updated blog and an active social media presence.

Your blog should exist on the same domain as your shopping cart. Your social media activities should reference your blog posts instead of being overly promotional. Potential customers will buy from you when they know, like, and trust your brand. Focus on delivering value to them and they'll be more than happy to choose your shop when they need what you're selling.

Keep Your Overhead to a Minimum

The whole appeal of running a drop shipping company is that there is minimal overhead. But if you don't watch your step, you could end up dealing with far more than you had bargained for. It's important that you have very clear terms of service when you're in the drop shipping business, as you're responsible for dealing with any issues related to customer complaints. Furthermore, consistent returns or complaints could result in the termination of your agreement with the supplier.

This doesn't imply that you should provide bad customer service. You just need to be extremely clear in what constitutes a valid return and what does not. You can minimize the chances of a requested return by providing clear and detailed descriptions of what the product does.

Drop Shipping isn't for Everyone

Even with the promise of reduced overhead, there's still a lot of work that needs to be done. For some, the allure of drop shipping turns out to be a false pretense. If you don't want to deal with customer service inquiries and constantly maintaining a blog or social media presence, there are other business opportunities worth considering.

If, however, you have always wanted to run your own shop but could never find the funds to get started, drop shipping might provide the perfect opportunity.

Make Money Selling Ebooks Online With Unique Marketing Strategy!

Did you know writing and selling ebooks have become one of the most profitable 'work at home' businesses on the Internet? Writing and selling ebooks can be extremely lucrative. Everyone looks for information on the Internet. If you can give them the kind of information they really want, they will be very happy to pay you for it. Learn from the prosperous about eBook marketing secrets to assure you of success.

There are many different ways to sell millions ebooks. If one of your goals is to become a **Millionaire or make a six-figure income online then consider selling ebooks by the quantity.** Most people just set a goal of making a million dollars over the Internet and that is good but most plans fall short of making that kind of income because making money is there only goal. When your goal of having your own home internet business that has that kind of success of earning one million dollars with the emphasis on selling a large number of units then your success will be very attainable.

The first thing you may want to consider is writing your own eBook and selling it online. There are plenty of topics on which you can write an ebook, just pick one that you are suited for. Ebooks are not that difficult to write and they do not take that long to write one. You can write an eBook in one day. Many ebooks are only about 25 pages. Some ebooks are about 200 pages. Just write about something that you already know. Think about your occupation or the hobbies that you have and you will realize that you are close to an expert on that subject.

If you only have one eBook that you want to sell in order to make a million dollars then you will have to sell one million ebooks making one-dollar profit on each one. This would be one of the hardest ways of selling one million ebooks. If your profit was 2 to 5 dollars on each eBook then you will not have to sell as many to make one million dollars.

Selling a million units with only one eBook title may take some years even if is a popular subject and well written that would appeal to a large audience or attract many consumers and customers. Although it is very possible to sell one million ebooks from just one title in a short period of time, most authors have a few ebooks to many ebooks for sale.

Your chances of selling one million ebooks increase dramatically when you have multiple titles that you are selling at the same time. If you have 30 ebooks that you have written and they are excellent ebooks and appeal to many customers then your goal of selling one million ebooks will increase greatly and much more quickly then selling just one title.

Use your imagination and try to conceive of having 100 to 1000 eBook titles that you could sell and how long it would take to sell one million ebooks. You can sell other author's ebooks and make a profit off of them, which will get you closer to your goal of selling many ebooks up to one million ebooks. Obviously the more eBook titles you have the closer you will be to your goal in selling one million ebooks.

Realistically you can have only 25 titles of ebooks that you have written or have purchased reseller rights on and sell one million ebooks in about a year. The key is to select the popular categories on what sells best on the Internet. Then the next thing you will need is to advertise it by using an eBook description that would make all people want to buy your ebook.

Check out this money making resource before you continue !

"Simply Copy & Paste" !
Click here to see This now

Highly Recommended Resources

"Simply Copy & Paste" !

Make Residual Passive Income Complete Done for you

Make $2000 Monthly on You tube

PLR Niche Guru

$1200 Cash Profit

Earn $1000 in 24 hours

Make Money with Facebook

Content Credits:

How to Make Money Online Fast in Today's Economy.
Article Source: http://EzineArticles.com/9379925

Genuine Ways Of Making Money Online
Article Source: http://EzineArticles.com/911908

Legitimate Ways to Make Money Online Fast
Article Source: http://EzineArticles.com/9340431

How to Make Money Online With Craigslist.
Article Source: http://EzineArticles.com/2497056

Make Money on You tube
Article Source: http://EzineArticles.com/7333255

Make money online with CPA offers.
Article Source: http://EzineArticles.com/2978145

Make Money Selling Ebooks Online With Unique Marketing Strategy!
Article Source: http://EzineArticles.com/1352203

www.ingramcontent.com/pod-product-compliance
Lightning Source LLC
Chambersburg PA
CBHW031505210526
45463CB00003B/1086